Paleo Lunch Box Recipes

50 Recipes for Making a Wholesome Yummylicious Lunchbox

Disclaimer

No part of this eBook can be transmitted or reproduced in any form including print, electronic, photocopying, scanning, mechanical or recording without prior written permission from the author.

While the author has taken utmost efforts to ensure the accuracy of the written content, all readers are advised to follow information mentioned herein at their own risk. The author cannot be held responsible for any personal or commercial damage caused by misinterpretation of information. All readers are encouraged to seek professional advice when needed.

What You Will Find In This Book?

Life has become unimaginably busy these days. Think how many times you missed breakfast last week. And if we talk about kids, they are usually so sleepy in the morning that they puke just by the thought of eating breakfast.

This is where why you, especially your kid needs to have a healthy hearty lunch. You might order a salad or sandwich, and give money to your kids to buy lunch for them, but this is definitely not a healthy approach.

So how about making a complete wholesome lunchbox for you and your kid; it is not that difficult after all. This cookbook will help you in doing that.

The "*50 Paleo Lunch Box Recipes*" contains the following.

1. Paleo lunch time recipes for kids and adults.
2. Recipes for Paleo dressings and dips to compliment the lunch box meals.
3. Paleo recipes for lunch time appetizers.
4. Paleo recipes for main course lunch meals.
5. Paleo desert recipes to complete the lunch box.
6. Nutritional facts along with every recipe.

Pick a recipe from every section and make your own healthy wholesome lunchbox.

Table of Contents

Disclaimer 2

What You Will Find In This Book? 3

Paleo Lunchbox Dips 12

  Chipotle Dip 12

    Serving Size 12

    Nutritional Facts (Values per Serving) 12

    Ingredients 12

    Preparation Method 12

  Classic Paleo Salsa 13

    Serving Size 13

    Nutritional Facts (Values per Serving) 13

    Ingredients 13

    Preparation Method 13

  Paleo Avocado Mayo Dip 14

    Serving Size 14

    Nutritional Facts (Values per Serving) 14

    Ingredients 14

    Preparation Method 14

  Paleo BBQ Sauce 15

    Serving Size 15

    Nutritional Facts (Values per Serving) 15

    Ingredients 15

    Preparation Method 15

  Jalapeno Tomato Sauce 17

    Serving Size 17

    Nutritional Facts (Values per Serving) 17

    Ingredients 17

    Preparation Method 17

  Paleo Hummus 19

    Serving Size 19

    Nutritional Facts (Values per Serving) 19

    Ingredients 19

    Preparation Method 19

Paleo Lunchbox Appetizers 20
Krispy Kale Chips 20
Serving Size 20
Nutritional Facts (Values per Serving) 20
Ingredients 20
Preparation Method 20
Spicy Avocado Salad 22
Serving Size 22
Nutritional Facts (Values per Serving) 22
Ingredients 22
Preparation Method 22
Paleo Sweet Crepes 23
Serving Size 23
Nutritional Facts (Values per Serving) 23
Ingredients 23
Preparation Method 23
Paleo Style Brussels Sprouts 24
Serving Size 24
Nutritional Facts (Values per Serving) 24
Ingredients 24
Preparation Method 24
Paleo Mexican Salad 25
Serving Size 25
Nutritional Facts (Values per Serving) 25
Ingredients 25
Preparation Method 26
Paleo Sweet Tuna Hash 27
Serving Size 27
Nutritional Facts (Values per Serving) 27
Ingredients 27
Preparation Method 27
Baked Chicken Wings 29
Serving Size 29
Nutritional Facts (Values per Serving) 29

- Ingredients 29
- Preparation Method 29
- Orange and Tuna Salad 31
  - Serving Size 31
  - Nutritional Facts (Values per Serving) 31
  - Ingredients 31
  - Preparation Method 31
- Ham Muffins 33
  - Serving Size 33
  - Nutritional Facts (Values per Serving) 33
  - Ingredients 33
  - Preparation Method 33
- Veggie Stir Fry Salad 34
  - Serving Size 34
  - Nutritional Facts (Values per Serving) 34
  - Ingredients 34
  - Preparation Method 34
- Citrus Jicama Salad 35
  - Serving Size 35
  - Nutritional Facts (Values per Serving) 35
  - Ingredients 35
  - Preparation Method 35
- Italian Bacon Crumble 37
  - Serving Size 37
  - Nutritional Facts (Values per Serving) 37
  - Ingredients 37
  - Preparation Method 37
- Paleo Caesar Salad 39
  - Serving Size 39
  - Nutritional Facts (Values per Serving) 39
  - Ingredients 39
  - Preparation Method 39

Paleo Lunchbox Main Course 41
- Tangy Grilled Chicken 41

- Serving Size 41
- Nutritional Facts (Values per Serving) 41
- Ingredients 41
- Preparation Method 41

Salmon Treat 42
- Serving Size 42
- Nutritional Facts (Values per Serving) 42
- Ingredients 42
- Preparation Method 42

Meaty Spaghetti Squash 44
- Serving Size 44
- Nutritional Facts (Values per Serving) 44
- Ingredients 44
- Preparation Method 45

Easy Pork Lunch 46
- Serving Size 46
- Nutritional Facts (Values per Serving) 46
- Ingredients 46
- Preparation Method 46

Andouille Jambalaya 48
- Serving Size 48
- Nutritional Facts (Values per Serving) 48
- Ingredients 48
- Preparation Method 48

Nut 'n' Cheese Chicken 50
- Serving Size 50
- Nutritional Facts (Values per Serving) 50
- Ingredients 50
- Preparation Method 50

Cheesilicious Paleo Pizza 52
- Serving Size 52
- Nutritional Facts (Values per Serving) 52
- Ingredients 52
- Preparation Method 52

- Spicy Tuna Burger 54
  - Serving Size 54
  - Nutritional Facts (Values per Serving) 54
  - Ingredients 54
  - Preparation Method 54
- Shrimp and Lemon Stir Fry 56
  - Serving Size 56
  - Nutritional Facts (Values per Serving) 56
  - Ingredients 56
  - Preparation Method 56
- Pepper and Pineapple Chicken 58
  - Serving Size 58
  - Nutritional Facts (Values per Serving) 58
  - Ingredients 58
  - Preparation Method 58
- Chicken 'n' Carrot Meat loaf 60
  - Serving Size 60
  - Nutritional Facts (Values per Serving) 60
  - Ingredients 60
  - Preparation Method 60
- Spicy Beef Delight 62
  - Serving Size 62
  - Nutritional Facts (Values per Serving) 62
  - Ingredients 62
  - Preparation Method 62
- Quick Walnut Squash 64
  - Serving Size 64
  - Nutritional Facts (Values per Serving) 64
  - Ingredients 64
  - Preparation Method 64
- Sweet 'n' Spicy Butternut Squash 65
  - Serving Size 65
  - Nutritional Facts (Values per Serving) 65
  - Ingredients 65

- Preparation Method 65
- Cauliflower Mint Rice 66
  - Serving Size 66
  - Nutritional Facts (Values per Serving) 66
  - Ingredients 66
  - Preparation Method 66
- Bacon and Sweet Potato Crumble 68
  - Serving Size 68
  - Nutritional Facts (Values per Serving) 68
  - Ingredients 68
  - Preparation Method 68
- Balsamic Grilled Chicken 70
  - Serving Size 70
  - Nutritional Facts (Values per Serving) 70
  - Ingredients 70
  - Preparation Method 70
- Paleo Crab Patties 72
  - Serving Size 72
  - Nutritional Facts (Values per Serving) 72
  - Ingredients 72
  - Preparation Method 72
- Drunken Fish with Red Sauce 74
  - Serving Size 74
  - Nutritional Facts (Values per Serving) 74
  - Ingredients 74
  - Preparation Method 74
- Spicy Sausage Burgers 76
  - Serving Size 76
  - Nutritional Facts (Values per Serving) 76
  - Ingredients 76
  - Preparation Method 76
- Melon and Pepper Grilled Shrimps 78
  - Serving Size 78
  - Nutritional Facts (Values per Serving) 78

- Ingredients 78
- Preparation Method 78

Sweet Paleo Lunchbox 80

Choco Coconut Smoothie 80
- Serving Size 80
- Nutritional Facts (Values per Serving) 80
- Ingredients 80
- Preparation Method 80

Apple 'n' Cranberries Cookies 81
- Serving Size 81
- Nutritional Facts (Values per Serving) 81
- Ingredients 81
- Preparation Method 81

Cashew Date Cookies 83
- Serving Size 83
- Nutritional Facts (Values per Serving) 83
- Ingredients 83
- Preparation Method 83

5-minute Ovenless Muffins 85
- Serving Size 85
- Nutritional Facts (Values per Serving) 85
- Ingredients 85
- Preparation Method 85

Choco Banana Loaf 86
- Serving Size 86
- Nutritional Facts (Values per Serving) 86
- Ingredients 86
- Preparation Method 86

Lemon 'n' Date Tarts 88
- Serving Size 88
- Nutritional Facts (Values per Serving) 88
- Ingredients for Tart Crust 88
- Ingredients for Tart Filling 88
- Preparation Method 88

Paleo Almond Bites 90
Serving Size 90
Nutritional Facts (Values per Serving) 90
Ingredients 90
Preparation Method 90
Fruit and Nut Bars 91
Serving Size 91
Nutritional Facts (Values per Serving) 91
Ingredients 91
Preparation Method 92
Fruity Coffee Cake 93
Serving Size 93
Nutritional Facts (Values per Serving) 93
Ingredients for Topping 93
Ingredients for Filling 93
Preparation Method 94
Applesauce Cupcakes 95
Serving Size 95
Nutritional Facts (Values per Serving) 95
Ingredients 95
Preparation Method 95

Paleo Lunchbox Dips

Chipotle Dip

Serving Size

Serves 8

Nutritional Facts (Values per Serving)

Calories/Serving: 133

Protein: 0.2 g

Cholesterol: 5 mg

Total Fat: 0.2 g

Total Carbohydrate: 1.3 g

Ingredients

Half cup – Paleo Mayonnaise

Half cup – fresh cilantro, chopped

1 Tbsp – fresh lime juice

2 – Chipotle peppers in adobo sauce

1 – Garlic Clove

2 Tbsp – Extra Virgin Olive Oil

Preparation Method

1. Blend all the ingredients in a food processor till it becomes a smooth puree.

You can serve it with any *Paleo Lunchbox Main Course* recipe.

Classic Paleo Salsa

Serving Size

Serves 4

Nutritional Facts (Values per Serving)

Calories/Serving: 30

Protein: 1.3 g

Total Fat: 0.3 g

Cholesterol: 0.1 mg

Total Carbohydrate: 6.7 g

Ingredients

6 – Italian plum tomatoes, chopped

1 Tbsp – fresh lime juice

1 – Jalapeno pepper, diced

1 cup – fresh cilantro, chopped

Half cup – chopped red onion

1 – Habanero pepper, diced

1 – Garlic clove, crushed

Salt and pepper to taste

Preparation Method

1. Blend all the ingredients in a food processor till it becomes a smooth puree.

You can serve it with tortillas, crepes and Kale chips.

Paleo Avocado Mayo Dip

Serving Size

Serves 16

Nutritional Facts (Values per Serving)

Calories/Serving: 125

Protein: 0.4 g

Total Fat: 13.9 g

Cholesterol: 13 mg

Total Carbohydrate: 0.2 g

Ingredients

1 ½ Tbsp – fresh lemon juice

Half cup – Olive oil

½ tsp – mustard powder

Half cup – Avocado oil

1 – Egg

¼ tsp – white pepper

Preparation Method

1. In a food processor, combine egg, mustard powder and lemon juice. Place the lid and blend till it becomes foamy.
2. Keep the blender running and remove the drip hole opening from the lid.
3. Start adding both the oils, drop by drop through the opening.
4. When all the oil is blended and it becomes a smooth puree, blend in white pepper.

Refrigerate in an air tight container when not in use.

Paleo BBQ Sauce

Serving Size

Serves 8

Nutritional Facts (Values per Serving)

Calories/Serving: 50

Protein: 1.8 g

Total Fat: 2.2 g

Cholesterol: 0 mg

Total Carbohydrate: 6.8 g

Ingredients

1 cup – Chicken stock

1 tsp – ground cumin

3 – Garlic cloves, crushed

1 tsp – ground black pepper

¼ cup – diced shallot

1 tsp – ground cayenne pepper

¾ cup – tomato paste

1 Tbsp – avocado oil

1 tsp – prepared horseradish

1 Tbsp – Dijon mustard

1 tsp – red pepper flakes

2 Tbsp – apple cider vinegar

½ tsp – salt

Preparation Method

1. Mix all the ingredients in a saucepan.

2. Bring it to simmer over medium heat, while stirring constantly.

3. Reduce the heat to low, cover the saucepan and let it simmer for 15 – 20 minutes or till the sauce thickens. Stir after every 3 – 4 minutes.

Jalapeno Tomato Sauce

Serving Size

Serve 10

Nutritional Facts (Values per Serving)

Calories/Serving: 15

Protein: 0.6 g

Total Fat: 0.1 g

Cholesterol: 0.1 mg

Total Carbohydrate: 3.4 g

Ingredients

6 – Italian plum tomatoes, cut in half

¼ cup – fresh cilantro, chopped

1 – Chipotle chili pepper, dried

1 – Small sized white onion, cut in quarters

1 – Garlic clove

1 Tbsp – fresh lime juice

1 – Jalapeno pepper, seeded and diced

Preparation Method

1. Soak the dried chipotle pepper in water for 15 minutes. Remove it from water and set aside.
2. Set the oven's broiler to preheat while placing the oven rack six inches above the heat.
3. Place aluminum foil in a baking sheet.
4. Line tomatoes in the aluminum-lined baking sheet.
5. Broil it for 12 – 15 minutes or till the skins of tomatoes are charred.
6. Flip the tomatoes and broil for another 5 minutes.

7. Put the charred tomatoes in a food processor along with all the other ingredients.

8. Blend till all the ingredients are thoroughly combined and it becomes a smooth puree.

Paleo Hummus

Serving Size

Serves 10

Nutritional Facts (Values per Serving)

Calories/Serving: 183

Protein: 5 g

Total Fat: 16 g

Cholesterol: 0.5 mg

Total Carbohydrate: 6 g

Ingredients

5 – Medium sized zucchini, peeled and diced

2 tsp – sea salt

2 Tbsp – fresh lemon juice

¾ cup – sesame tahini

1 Tbsp – ground cumin

¼ cup – olive oil

4 – Garlic cloves (peeled and crushed)

¼ teaspoon – paprika

Preparation Method

1. Peel and chop the zucchinis.
2. Put it in a food processor along with all the other ingredients, except for paprika.
3. Blend till it becomes a smooth paste.
4. Take it out in a bowl. Garnish with paprika and serve.

Paleo Lunchbox Appetizers

Krispy Kale Chips

Serving Size

Serves 3 – 4

Nutritional Facts (Values per Serving)

Calories/Serving: 110

Protein: 5.1 g

Total Fat: 5 g

Cholesterol: 0 mg

Total Carbohydrate: 16 g

Ingredients

1 Tbsp – Olive Oil

1 large bunch – Kale, pat dry on a paper towel

Salt and pepper to taste

Preparation Method

1. Set the oven to preheat at 400°F.
2. Remove the tough stems of the Kale and tear it into large random pieces.
3. Put all the kale pieces in a large bowl.
4. Drizzle with olive oil.
5. Season the kale with salt and pepper.
6. Use your hand to mix the kale so that all pieces get coated with oil, salt and pepper.
7. Spread the kale on a baking sheet. Make sure the leaves do not overlap. Bake in two batches if needed.
8. Put it in the preheated oven for 8 – 12 minutes or till the leaves becomes crispy.

Spicy Avocado Salad

Serving Size

Serves 6

Nutritional Facts (Values per Serving)

Calories/Serving: 118

Protein: 1.7 g

Total Fat: 9.9 g

Cholesterol: 0 mg

Total Carbohydrate: 8.2 g

Ingredients

1 Tbsp – fresh lime juice

Half cup – minced onion

2 – Avocados, peeled and pitted

1 – Jalapeno pepper, chopped

1 – Italian plum tomato, chopped

1 – Garlic clove, crushed

1 Tbsp – chopped cilantro

Salt and pepper to taste

Preparation Method

1. Put avocados in a bowl.
2. Pour lime juice over it.
3. Mash the avocados with a fork.
4. Add all the remaining ingredients
5. Mix and serve.

Serve with any of the Paleo Lunchbox Dips.

Paleo Sweet Crepes

Serving Size

Makes 6 crepes

Nutritional Facts (Values per Serving)

Calories/Serving: 118

Protein: 9 g

Total Fat: 7.2 g

Cholesterol: 180 mg

Total Carbohydrate: 5.1 g

Ingredients

5 – Eggs

2 tsp – butter

Half cup – almond flour

2 tsp – honey

Pinch of salt

Preparation Method

1. In a large bowl, combine all the ingredients, except butter. Mix well.
2. Divide the mixture evenly into 6 parts and form a ball of each part. Now you will have 6 balls.
3. Press each ball to make a crepe of it.
4. Heat butter in a nonstick pan over medium heat.
5. Cook each crepe in the hot pan for about 2 minutes on each side, or till it becomes light brown.

Serve it hot!

Paleo Style Brussels Sprouts

Serving Size

Serves 3 – 4

Nutritional Facts (Values per Serving)

Calories/Serving: 88

Protein: 4 g

Total Fat: 4.1 g

Cholesterol: 0.2 mg

Total Carbohydrate: 11 g

Ingredients

1 lb. – Brussels sprouts, trimmed

½ tsp – dried thyme

1 Tbsp – extra virgin olive oil

1 cup – vegetable broth

¼ tsp – pepper

2 – Shallots, sliced

¼ tsp – salt

Preparation Method

1. Heat olive oil in a nonstick pan over medium heat.
2. Sauté shallots and Brussels sprouts in it till both the ingredients are starting to brown, while stirring frequently.
3. Add salt, dried thyme, vegetable broth and pepper in it.
4. Cover the pan and reduce the heat to low.
5. Let it cook for another 10 – 15 minutes or till the sprouts become tender.

Enjoy the wholesome Paleo Style Brussels Sprouts

Paleo Mexican Salad

Serving Size

Serves 4

Nutritional Facts (Values per Serving)

Calories/Serving: 385

Protein: 25 g

Total Fat: 24.7 g

Cholesterol: 83 mg

Total Carbohydrate: 18.5 g

Ingredients

3 cups – cherry tomatoes, cut into halves

2 tsp – ground cumin

½ tsp – cayenne pepper

1 lb. – ground beef

2 – Garlic cloves, crushed

¼ cup – sour cream

2 – Romaine hearts, grated or finely chopped

¼ cup – Cheddar cheese, grated

2 Tbsp – red chili powder

2 tsp – garlic powder

1 – Medium sized onion, chopped

Half cup – salsa sauce

1 Tbsp – lime juice

1/3 cup – fresh cilantro, diced

Salt and pepper to taste

Preparation Method

1. In a bowl, combine cumin, chili powder, salt, cayenne pepper, pepper and garlic powder. Mix well and set aside.
2. Heat a nonstick pan over medium heat.
3. Brown the meat in it.
4. Stir in garlic and onion. Cook till the onion becomes translucent.
5. Stir in the spice mixture and cook for another 2 – 3 minutes.
6. In another bowl, put salsa, lime juice and sour cream. Mix well.
7. To serve, spread the romaine lettuce on the serving plate.
8. Put the cooked meat on top of it.
9. Pour over the salsa mixture.
10. Top it up with cherry tomatoes, cheese and cilantro. Enjoy!

Paleo Sweet Tuna Hash

Serving Size

Serves 3

Nutritional Facts (Values per Serving)

Calories/Serving: 458

Protein: 33.2 g

Total Fat: 16 g

Cholesterol: 87 mg

Total Carbohydrate: 48.7 g

Ingredients

¾ cup – almond flour

1 Tbsp – baking powder

6 oz. – canned tuna

1 cup – pineapple, chopped

¼ cup – almond milk

Half cup – coconut flour

1 – Egg

¼ cup – Orange juice

2 Tbsp – Olive oil

Preparation Method

1. In a large mixing bowl, combine all the ingredients expect olive oil. Whisk well till it becomes a batter.

2. Heat oil in a nonstick skillet over medium heat.

3. Pour over a scoop of this batter in the skillet and let it cook for about 3 minutes.

4. Flip over and cook again for 3 minutes.

5. Cook for a total of 15 minutes while flipping after 3 minutes or till the hash patty becomes crispy.

6. Perform the same with the remaining batter.

Serve with any of the *Paleo Lunch Box Dips.*

Baked Chicken Wings

Serving Size

Serves 5 – 6

Nutritional Facts (Values per Serving)

Calories/Serving: 313

Protein: 27.9 g

Total Fat: 15.1 g

Cholesterol: 93 mg

Total Carbohydrate: 13.4 g

Ingredients

2 lbs. – chicken breast, skinless and boneless

1 – Medium sized yellow onion, chopped

4 – Garlic cloves, chopped

1 Tbsp – Extra virgin olive oil

1 bulb – fennel, diced

½ tsp – fennel seeds

1 – Dried chile de arbol pepper

28 oz. – canned whole peeled tomatoes in puree

Half cup – white wine

½ Tbsp – dried thyme

Half cup – Castelvetrano olives, pitted and cut into halves

Salt and pepper to taste

Fresh chopped parsley to garnish

Preparation Method

1. Set the oven to preheat at 350°F.

2. Heat oil in an oven proof skillet over medium – high heat.

3. Coat the chicken breasts with salt and pepper.

4. Cook the chicken breasts in the heated skillet for five minutes each side or till it becomes brown.

5. Take it out in a bowl.

6. Reduce the heat of the skillet to medium and put onion and fennel seeds in it. Cook till both the ingredients starts to caramelize. This should take about 10 minutes.

7. Stir in thyme, garlic and chile de arbol pepper. Cook for another minute.

8. Stir in the white wine and tomatoes with puree. Bring it to a boil.

9. Break the tomatoes with a wooden spatula and mix well.

10. Finally, add chicken thighs and olives in it. Stir to mix.

11. Put it in the preheated oven for 40 – 45 minutes or until the chickens is no longer pink from inside.

12. Set aside to cool for 5 – 10 minutes.

13. Garnish with fresh parsley and serve.

Orange and Tuna Salad

Serving Size

Serves 3 – 4

Nutritional Facts (Values per Serving)

Calories/Serving: 208

Protein: 29 g

Total Fat: 4 g

Cholesterol: 44 mg

Total Carbohydrate: 13 g

Ingredients

1 lb. – tuna steaks, 1 inch thick, cut into four pieces

3 – Medium sized oranges

½ tsp – ground coriander

1 Tbsp – rice vinegar

1 Tbsp – canola oil

¼ tsp – cayenne pepper

1 tsp – crystallized ginger

½ tsp – aniseed, chopped

1 cup – small watercress sprigs

¼ tsp – pepper

½ tsp – kosher salt

Preparation Method

1. Peel and remove the white pith of the oranges. Carefully remove the membranes of the slices and put all the orange meat in a bowl

2. Add rice vinegar, oil, ground coriander, ginger, cayenne pepper, half of the aniseed and half of salt.

3. Stir in the watercress sprigs in the orange salad mixture. Mix well and set aside.

4. Set oven to preheat at high while adjusting the oven rack at least 5 inches above the broiler.

5. Line a broiler pan with aluminum foil.

6. Season tuna steak with pepper and the remaining salt and aniseed.

7. Put it on the prepared broiler pan.

8. Broil on medium for 4 minutes each side.

9. To serve, put the broiled tuna on a serving plate. Top it up with orange salad.

Ham Muffins

Serving Size

Makes 4 muffins

Nutritional Facts (Values per Serving)

Calories/Serving: 308

Protein: 23.8 g

Total Fat: 20.5 g

Cholesterol: 254 mg

Total Carbohydrate: 6.8 g

Ingredients

4 – Eggs

Half cup – chopped red bell pepper

Pinch of salt

Half cup – chopped onion

Pinch of black pepper

4 oz. – ham, cooked and crumbled

1 Tbsp – water

Preparation Method

1. Set the oven to preheat at 350°F.
2. Line a muffin baking pan with paper liners.
3. In a large bowl, beat eggs.
4. Beat in all the other ingredients.
5. Pour out the batter in the paper-lined muffin pan while filling ¾ of each muffin tin.
6. Put the pan in the preheated oven for 18 – 20 minutes or until cooked through.

Veggie Stir Fry Salad

Serving Size

Serves 3 – 4

Nutritional Facts (Values per Serving)

Calories/Serving: 107

Protein: 3 g

Total Fat: 4 g

Cholesterol: 0.1 mg

Total Carbohydrate: 17 g

Ingredients

4 cups – mixed frozen vegetables

1 Tbsp – Extra virgin olive oil

½ tsp – dried dill

1 – Shallot, finely chopped

Salt and pepper to taste

Preparation Method

1. Heat olive oil in a nonstick pan over medium heat.
2. Sauté shallot for about a minute or till it becomes soft, while stirring constantly.
3. Add the frozen vegetables.
4. Cover the pan and cook for 5 minutes or till the veggies get tender, while stirring frequently.
5. Stir in salt, pepper and dill.

The healthy Veggie Stir Fry Salad is ready to devour.

Citrus Jicama Salad

Serving Size

Serves 3 – 4

Nutritional Facts (Values per Serving)

Calories/Serving: 138

Protein: 3 g

Total Fat: 7 g

Cholesterol: 0.1 mg

Total Carbohydrate: 17.1 g

Ingredients

1 – Small sized jicama, peeled and cut into thin strips

4 oz. – snow peas, trimmed

1 Tbsp – minced shallot

2 Tbsp – extra virgin olive oil

1 tsp – sugar

2 – Oranges

3 Tbsp – fresh orange juice

1 Tbsp – white wine vinegar

¼ tsp – salt

Preparation Method

1. Fit a steamer basket in a saucepan.
2. Fill water up to 1 inch and bring it to a boil.
3. Put the snow peas in the boiling water.
4. Steam for about 3 minutes or till the peas become tender.
5. Pour out the peas in a bowl of ice cold water.

6. Peel the oranges and remove all the white pith.
7. Remove the membrane of all the orange slices.
8. In a bowl, whisk together orange juice, oil, shallot, vinegar, salt and sugar.
9. Add orange slices in it. Stir to combine.
10. Stir in the drained snow peas and jicama.
11. Serve with any of the Paleo Lunchbox Dips.

Italian Bacon Crumble

Serving Size

Serves 3 – 4

Nutritional Facts (Values per Serving)

Calories/Serving: 124

Protein: 3 g

Total Fat: 9 g

Cholesterol: 5 mg

Total Carbohydrate: 8 g

Ingredients

4 cups – cauliflower florets, chopped

1 tablespoon – garlic paste

2 Tbsp – pancetta, chopped

2 Tbsp – water

1 cup – grape tomatoes, cut into halves

2 Tbsp – extra virgin olive oil

2 tsp – red wine vinegar

2 Tbsp – fresh parsley, chopped

¼ tsp – pepper

¼ tsp – salt

Preparation Method

1. Brown pancetta in a nonstick skillet over medium heat.
2. Pat dry the pancetta on paper towel.
3. Heat one tablespoon olive oil in a nonstick pan over medium heat.

4. Add cauliflower florets in the pan, cover the pan and let it cook for 4 minutes while stirring occasionally.

5. Stir in vinegar and water. Cover it again and cook for another 4 minutes.

6. Add the remaining oil and all the remaining ingredients in the pan and cook for 2 -3 minutes.

7. Serve with cooked pancetta.

Paleo Caesar Salad

Serving Size

Serves 2

Nutritional Facts (Values per Serving)

Calories/Serving: 168

Protein: 6.6 g

Total Fat: 12.5 g

Cholesterol: 0 mg

Total Carbohydrate: 11.1 g

Ingredients

1 – Avocado

1 Tbsp – caper brine

2 Tbsp – water

1 Tbsp – capers

3 Tbsp – fresh lemon juice

3 – Garlic cloves, crushed

2 tsp – Dijon mustard

Sea salt and pepper to taste

12 cups – romaine leaves, coarsely chopped

1/4 cup – hemp seeds

Preparation Method

1. Blend the first 8 ingredients in a food processor. Keep blending till it forms a smoothie.

2. Put romaine leaves in a serving bowl.

3. Pour out the smoothie over the leaves.

4. Drizzle with hemp seeds and serve.

Paleo Lunchbox Main Course

Tangy Grilled Chicken

Serving Size

Serves 4

Nutritional Facts (Values per Serving)

Calories/Serving: 136

Protein: 23 g

Total Fat: 4 g

Cholesterol: 63 mg

Total Carbohydrate: 1.1 g

Ingredients

1 lb – chicken breast, skinless and boneless

2 Tbsp – extra virgin olive oil

1 – Medium sized onion, finely chopped

2 Tbsp – allspice

¼ cup – fresh lime juice

1 tsp – salt

Cooking spray

Preparation Method

1. In a large bowl, combine lime juice, onion, salt, oil and allspice. Mix well.
2. Marinade the chicken breasts with the lime mixture and set aside for 1 hour.
3. Preheat a broiler and grease the broiler tray with cooking spray.
4. Place the chicken breasts on the prepared broiler tray.
5. Broil it for 10 – 15 minutes or until cooked through, while flipping the chicken once in between. Enjoy!

Salmon Treat

Serving Size

Serves 4

Nutritional Facts (Values per Serving)

Calories/Serving: 248

Protein: 35 g

Total Fat: 10 g

Cholesterol: 80 mg

Total Carbohydrate: 3 g

Ingredients

1 - Wild salmon fillet (about 1 - 1 ½ lbs)

2 – Medium sized tomatoes, finely sliced

2 – Garlic cloves, crushed

1 Tbsp – extra virgin olive oil

1 cup - fresh basil, finely chopped

¼ tsp – pepper

1 tsp – sea salt

Cooking spray

Preparation Method

1. Set the griller to preheat at medium.
2. In a bowl, combine oil, minced garlic and salt.
3. Grease a large double layer of aluminum foil with cooking spray.
4. Place the salmon fillet over it, skin side down.
5. Brush the garlic mixture over it.
6. Spread tomatoes and half of the basil on top of it.

7. Put it in the preheated grill.
8. Grill for about 12 minutes or till the fish flakes easily.
9. Place it on the serving tray and garnish with the remaining basil.

Meaty Spaghetti Squash

Serving Size

Serves 7 – 8

Nutritional Facts (Values per Serving)

Calories/Serving: 388

Protein: 17 g

Total Fat: 29.9 g

Cholesterol: 52 mg

Total Carbohydrate: 14.5 g

Ingredients

1 – Spaghetti squash, seeded and cut in half

1 – Medium sized white onion, chopped

1 cup – mushrooms, sliced

1 – Green bell pepper, diced

22 oz. – canned crushed tomatoes

¼ cup – fresh oregano, chopped

1 Tbsp – red pepper flakes

¼ cup – water

1 ½ lb – ground beef

1 Tbsp – extra virgin olive oil

1 – Zucchini, chopped

1 – Red bell pepper, diced

¼ cup – fresh basil, chopped

Half cup – extra virgin olive oil

¼ cup – fresh thyme, chopped

Preparation Method

1. Set the oven to preheat at 400°F.

2. Pour water in a baking tray.

3. Put squash halves in the water and put it in the preheated oven for 30 – 40 minutes, or till squash become tender.

4. Meanwhile, cook beef and onion in a nonstick pan over medium-high heat. Cook till the beef becomes crumbly and light brown. Set aside.

5. In another nonstick pan, heat one tablespoon oil over medium heat.

6. Sauté mushrooms, green bell peppers, zucchini and red bell peppers in it.

7. Stir in crushed tomatoes, oregano, basil and thyme in it. Simmer it over medium heat for 10 minutes.

8. Now add cooked beef and onion in it. Mix well.

9. Reduce the heat to low and let it simmer for a few more minutes while stirring occasionally.

10. When the squash is cooked through, shred it using two forks.

11. Put it in the meat containing pan. Stir to combine.

12. Take it out on the serving plate.

13. Drizzle with the remaining olive oil and serve.

Easy Pork Lunch

Serving Size

Serves 4

Nutritional Facts (Values per Serving)

Calories/Serving: 308

Protein: 22.4 g

Total Fat: 18 g

Cholesterol: 63 mg

Total Carbohydrate: 14.4 g

Ingredients

1 lb – pork tenderloin, cut into thin slices

½ cup – fresh cilantro, finely chopped

4 – Garlic cloves, chopped

2 Tbsp – olive pomace oil

1 – Red bell pepper, cut into thin slices

¼ cup – Extra virgin olive oil

1 Tbsp – chopped ginger

2 – Medium sized onions, finely sliced

1 Tbsp – fresh lime juice

Chopped fresh cilantro to garnish

Preparation Method

1. In a large bowl, combine extra virgin olive oil, cilantro, ginger and garlic. Mix well.
2. Toss the pork strips in it. Mix well.
3. Set it aside to marinade for at least an hour.
4. Heat one tablespoon olive pomace oil in a saucepan.

5. Brown the marinated pork in it.
6. In another pan, heat the remaining olive pomace oil.
7. Sauté onion slices in it.
8. Stir in bell pepper and cook for 3 – 4 minutes while stirring constantly.
9. Stir in cooked pork.
10. Stir in lime juice. Cook for another minute and then serve.

Andouille Jambalaya

Serving Size

Serves 5 – 6

Nutritional Facts (Values per Serving)

Calories/Serving: 260

Protein: 31.8 g

Total Fat: 8.5 g

Cholesterol: 167 mg

Total Carbohydrate: 14.5 g

Ingredients

1 lb – shrimp (cooked, peeled and deveined)

1 Tbsp – butter

2 – andouille sausage, cut into ¼ inch pieces

14 oz. – canned crushed tomatoes

2 – Zucchinis, chopped

1 lb – chicken breast, cooked and diced

1 tsp – hot sauce

1 Tbsp – olive oil

1 – Large sized onion, chopped

6 – Garlic cloves, diced

3 – Green bell peppers, seeded and chopped

2 Tbsp – Cajun seasoning

1 cup – chicken broth

Preparation Method

1. In a saucepan, heat oil and butter over medium heat.

2. Brown onion and andouille sausage in it.
3. Stir in garlic and cook for 2 minutes.
4. Stir in green bell peppers, crushed tomatoes, Cajun seasoning, zucchinis, chicken broth and hot sauce. Bring it to a boil.
5. Reduce the heat to low and simmer for about 15 minutes, or till the mixture starts to thicken.
6. Finally, add chicken and shrimps in it. Cook for another 2 minutes.

The delectable Andouille Jambalaya is ready to serve.

Nut 'n' Cheese Chicken

Serving Size

Serves 3 – 4

Nutritional Facts (Values per Serving)

Calories/Serving: 637

Protein: 36.8 g

Total Fat: 52.8 g

Cholesterol: 93 mg

Total Carbohydrate: 7.4 g

Ingredients

2 – Chicken breasts, skinless and boneless, cut into horizontal halves

8 – Slices of bacon

8 oz. – blue cheese, crumbled

6 oz. – walnuts, break into halves

Preparation Method

1. Set the oven to preheat at 350°F.
2. Flatten the chicken slices with meat mallet.
3. Spread cheese and walnuts on each chicken slice. Roll over the chicken slice.
4. Roll a bacon slice over each chicken roll.
5. Secure the roll with toothpicks.
6. Heat a nonstick pan to medium heat.
7. Brown the bacon wrapped chicken rolls in it. This should take About 5 minutes.
8. Place the rolls on the baking tray.
9. Bake for 30 – 35 minutes or till the chicken is cooked through.

Serve with any of the *Paleo Lunch box Dips*.

Cheesilicious Paleo Pizza

Serving Size

Serves 5 – 6

Nutritional Facts (Values per Serving)

Calories/Serving: 506

Protein: 56.5 g

Total Fat: 27.8 g

Cholesterol: 229 mg

Total Carbohydrate: 5.1 g

Ingredients

2 lbs – lean ground beef

1 tsp – caraway seeds

1 tsp – garlic salt

1 tsp – red pepper flakes

Half cup – Parmesan cheese, grated

1 cup – tomato sauce

1 Tbsp – sea salt

1 tsp – dried oregano

1 tsp – ground black pepper

2 – Eggs

Half cup – mozzarella cheese, grated

3 ½ oz. – packaged sliced pepperoni

Preparation Method

1. Set the oven to preheat at 450°F.
2. Coat a 12 x 17 inch round pizza pan with cooking spray.

3. In a small bowl, combine salt, oregano, caraway seeds, black pepper, garlic salt and red pepper flakes. Mix well and set aside.

4. In another large mixing bowl, combine beef and eggs. Mix thoroughly.

5. Mix in parmesan cheese and spice mixture.

6. Press the beef mixture evenly into the prepared pizza pan

7. Put it in the preheated oven for 10 minutes or until the meat is no longer pink.

8. Adjust the oven rack 6 inches over the heat.

9. Turn on the oven's broiler.

10. Sprinkle one-third of mozzarella cheese over the baked meat.

11. Spread an even layer of tomato sauce over.

12. Sprinkle another one-third of mozzarella cheese over the tomato sauce.

13. Place the pepperoni slices over it.

14. Finally, top it up with the remaining mozzarella cheese.

15. Broil for 4 – 5 minutes or till the cheese melts and becomes light brown.

Spicy Tuna Burger

Serving Size

Makes 4 burger patties

Nutritional Facts (Values per Serving)

Calories/Serving: 340

Protein: 39.8 g

Total Fat: 17.4 g

Cholesterol: 193 mg

Total Carbohydrate: 6 g

Ingredients

8 oz. – canned tuna, drained

Half cup – almond meal

¼ cup – fresh cilantro, chopped

2 Tbsp – lemon juice

3 – Eggs

2 Tbsp – soy sauce

2 Tbsp – olive oil

1 Tbsp – grated ginger root

Sea salt and black pepper to taste

Olive oil for frying (about 1 Tbsp)

Preparation Method

1. In a large bowl, combine tuna, cilantro, soy sauce, olive oil, ginger, lemon juice, eggs, salt, almond meal and pepper. Mix well.

2. Divide the mixture into 4 equal parts.

3. Form a burger patty of each part of the tuna mixture

4. Heat about one tablespoon olive oil in a skillet over medium heat.

5. Fry the tuna patties in it for about 5 minutes on each side, or till it becomes brown and crispy.

Serve with tomato ketchup and hamburger buns.

Shrimp and Lemon Stir Fry

Serving Size

Makes 24 large shrimps

Nutritional Facts (Values per Serving)

Calories/Serving: 388

Protein: 21.1 g

Total Fat: 31.7 g

Cholesterol: 192 mg

Total Carbohydrate: 5.8 g

Ingredients

24 – Large shrimps, peeled and deveined

1 – Small sized onion, finely diced

3 – Garlic cloves, crushed

1 Tbsp – grated ginger

Half cup – fresh lemon juice

Half cup – olive oil

1 Tbsp – lemon zest

1 tsp – ground turmeric

1 Tbsp – coconut oil

Preparation Method

1. In a bowl, combine lemon juice, olive oil, lemon zest, onion, garlic, ginger and turmeric. Mix well.

2. Add shrimps in this bowl and mix thoroughly so that all the shrimps get properly coated with the marinade.

3. Cover the bowl and put it in the refrigerator for at least 2 hours (maximum overnight).

4. Heat coconut oil in a skillet over medium-high heat.//
5. Add the shrimps in it. Do no put the marinade yet.
6. Stir fry the shrimps for about 10 minutes or till the shrimps becomes pink.
7. Add the marinade in it and bring it to a boil while stirring constantly.

The delicious Shrimp and Lemon Stir Fry is ready to devour.

Pepper and Pineapple Chicken

Serving Size

Serves 5 – 6

Nutritional Facts (Values per Serving)

Calories/Serving: 309

Protein: 18.3 g

Total Fat: 6.7 g

Cholesterol: 43 mg

Total Carbohydrate: 47.3 g

Ingredients

2 – Large chicken breasts, skinless and boneless, cut into cubes

2 Tbsp – chopped ginger

1 – Large sized onion

1 cup – pineapple cubes

2 Tbsp – extra virgin olive oil

¾ cup – honey

2 – Red bell peppers, diced

1 – Large head of broccoli

Preparation Method

1. Cut the onion into 8 wedges.
2. Cut the broccoli into florets.
3. Heat olive oil in a saucepan over medium heat.
4. Put the chicken cubes, ginger and half of the honey in it.
5. Cook for about 10 minutes or till the chicken becomes brown, while stirring occasionally.

6. Stir in the remaining ingredients and vegetables.

7. Cover the pan and let it cook on medium-high heat for about 8 minutes or till the veggies are tender, while stirring occasionally. Enjoy!

Chicken 'n' Carrot Meat loaf

Serving Size

Makes 6 – 8

Nutritional Facts (Values per Serving)

Calories/Serving: 123

Protein: 15.3 g

Total Fat: 3.3 g

Cholesterol: 134 mg

Total Carbohydrate: 8.1 g

Ingredients

7 – Chicken tenderloins

1 – Celery stalk

2 – Garlic cloves

1 tsp – ground black pepper

4 – Eggs

6 – Carrots

1 – Small sized onion

1 Tbsp – Italian seasoning

8 oz. – sodium less tomato sauce

Cooking Spray

Preparation Method

1. Set the oven to preheat at 350°F.
2. Coat a 9x5 inch loaf pan with cooking spray.
3. Combine celery, carrots, garlic, onion, black pepper and Italian seasoning in a food processor. Blend till all the ingredients are thoroughly minced and combined.

4. Take it out in a large bowl. Whisk in eggs.//
5. Stir in half of the tomato sauce. Mix well.
6. Now add chicken cubes in the food processor. Pulse until chicken is thoroughly grinded.
7. Fold the ground chicken into the vegetable-tomato blend.
8. Pour it into the greased loaf pan.
9. Put it in the preheated oven for 90 minutes.
10. Spread the remaining sauce over the loaf.
11. Bake it for another 30 minutes or until cooked through.
12. Set aside to cool for 20 minutes.
13. Slice and serve.

Spicy Beef Delight

Serving Size

Makes 4 – 5

Nutritional Facts (Values per Serving)

Calories/Serving: 68

Protein: 2.7 g

Total Fat: 2.9 g

Cholesterol: 0.1 mg

Total Carbohydrate: 8.5 g

Ingredients

2 ½ lb. – London broil roast beef, sliced

1/3 cup – hot water

1 Tbsp – liquid smoke flavoring

1 Tbsp – garlic powder

1 ½ tsp – Creole seasoning

2/3 cup – soy sauce

¼ cup – Worcestershire sauce

1 Tbsp – onion powder

1 ½ tsp – cayenne pepper

1 ½ tsp – Cajun seasoning

Preparation Method

1. In a microwave safe bowl, combine hot water, soy sauce, Creole seasoning, liquid smoke flavoring, Worcestershire sauce, garlic powder, onion powder, cayenne pepper and Cajun seasoning. Whisk well.

2. Microwave for 60 seconds. Stir to combine.

3. Stir in roast beef. Cover the bowl and put it in the refrigerator to marinade for at least 4 hours (maximum overnight).

4. Set the oven to preheat at 160°F.

5. Put the beef slices in the oven rack, at least one inch apart each other.

6. Let it dehydrate in the oven for about 6 hours or until the desired beef dryness is achieved.

Quick Walnut Squash

Serving Size

Serves 2

Nutritional Facts (Values per Serving)

Calories/Serving: 556

Protein: 11.2 g

Total Fat: 53.6 g

Cholesterol: 0.2 mg

Total Carbohydrate: 17.6 g

Ingredients

1 cup – walnuts, coarsely chopped

2 Tbsp – coconut oil

1 – Large sized tomato, cut into large pieces

3 – Garlic cloves, crushed

1 – Yellow squash, shredded

Preparation Method

1. Heat coconut oil in a nonstick pan over medium heat.
2. Stir in tomato, squash, walnuts and garlic in it.
3. Cook for 5 minutes while stirring constantly.

Serve!

Sweet 'n' Spicy Butternut Squash

Serving Size

Serves 2

Nutritional Facts (Values per Serving)

Calories/Serving: 424

Protein: 11.8 g

Total Fat: 6.6 g

Cholesterol: 15 mg

Total Carbohydrate: 91.3 g

Ingredients

1 – Butternut squash, peeled and cut into cubes

1 mango, peeled and cut into cubes

3 – Bacon slices

1 tsp – dried thyme

Salt and pepper to taste

Preparation Method

1. Cut the bacon slices into ¼ inch squares.
2. Brown the bacon pieces in a large nonstick pan.
3. Stir in thyme and squash. Cook and stir for about 20 minutes or till the squash becomes light brown.
4. Stir in mango cubes. Cook for another 5 minutes while stirring constantly.

Enjoy!

Cauliflower Mint Rice

Serving Size

Serves 5 – 6

Nutritional Facts (Values per Serving)

Calories/Serving: 120

Protein: 2.3 g

Total Fat: 9.5 g

Cholesterol: 0.1 mg

Total Carbohydrate: 8 g

Ingredients

¼ cup – fresh lemon juice

Half – Red bell pepper, finely chopped

3 Tbsp – fresh mint leaves, chopped

1 – Small sized yellow onion, finely chopped

1 – Cauliflower head

Half cup – grape tomatoes, cut into halves

¼ cup – extra virgin olive oil

Salt and black pepper to taste

Preparation Method

1. Cut the cauliflower into large florets.
2. In a bowl, combine onion and lemon juice. Let it sit for 30 minutes so that the lemon juice absorbs the flavor and smell of onion.
3. Drain the onion and keep the lemon juice in another bowl.
4. Pulse the cauliflower florets in a food processor till it takes the form of rice.
5. Heat a nonstick pan over medium heat. Put the cauliflower rice in it.

6. Cover and let it cook for 10 minutes or till the cauliflower is steamed while stirring occasionally.

7. Stir in bell pepper and grape tomatoes.

8. Cook and stir for another 3 minutes.

9. Stir in chopped mint leaves and onion. Cool and stir for two more minutes. Take it out in a large bowl.

10. In another bowl, combine olive oil, salt, onion flavored lemon juice and pepper. Mix well.

11. Pour it over the cauliflower rice. Stir to combine.

Serve!

Bacon and Sweet Potato Crumble

Serving Size

Serves 7 – 8

Nutritional Facts (Values per Serving)

Calories/Serving: 237

Protein: 5.8 g

Total Fat: 14.8 g

Cholesterol: 21 mg

Total Carbohydrate: 21.5 g

Ingredients

5 – Slices of uncured bacon, chopped

2 cups – chicken broth

¼ cup – roasted almonds

1 Tbsp – lemon juice

3 – Sweet potatoes, peeled and cubed

3 Tbsp – butter

1 cup – fresh basil leaves

3 Tbsp – Extra virgin olive oil

Salt and black pepper to taste

¾ cup – milk

Preparation Method

1. Combine sweet potatoes and chicken broth in a saucepan. Bring it to a boil over medium heat.

2. Reduce the heat to low, cover the pan and let it simmer for about 10 minutes or till the potatoes are tender.

3. Drain the potatoes and put it back in the pan.

4. Add butter in the pan and place a lid over it.

5. Brown the bacon in a nonstick skillet over medium heat. Absorb its grease on a paper towel and set aside.

6. Combine roasted almonds and basil in a food processor. Pulse for 30 seconds.

7. Keep the processor running and start adding olive oil in it, drop by drop.

8. Pulse for about 2 minutes or till the mixture thickens.

9. Add in it, salt, pepper and lemon juice. Blend for few more minutes to combine all the ingredients.

10. Mash the sweet potatoes with a fork. Add milk and whisk to combine.

11. Stir in bacon and almond mixture.

12. Mix well and serve immediately.

Balsamic Grilled Chicken

Serving Size

Serves 4

Nutritional Facts (Values per Serving)

Calories/Serving: 170

Protein: 23 g

Total Fat: 7 g

Cholesterol: 63 mg

Total Carbohydrate: 1 g

Ingredients

1 ¼ lbs. – chicken breast, skinless and boneless

¼ cup – extra virgin olive oil

2 – Garlic cloves, crushed

1 tsp – salt

¼ cup – balsamic vinegar

1 Tbsp – Italian seasoning

½ tsp – ground black pepper

Cooking spray

Preparation Method

1. In a large bowl, combine vinegar, oil, salt, garlic, pepper and Italian seasoning.
2. Toss the chicken breasts in it. Mix well so that every part of chicken gets thoroughly coated with the marinade.
3. Cover the bowl and put it in the refrigerator to marinade for 1 hour.
4. Preheat the broiler to medium-high.
5. Coat a broiler pan with cooking spray.

6. Place the marinated chicken in the prepared broiler pan.

7. Broil it for 10 – 15 minutes or till an instant-read thermometer when inserted into the chicken reads 165°F. Make sure to flip the chicken once in between.

The wholesome Balsamic Grilled Chicken is ready to serve.

Paleo Crab Patties

Serving Size

Serves 6

Nutritional Facts (Values per Serving)

Calories/Serving: 177

Protein: 22.4 g

Total Fat: 7.5 g

Cholesterol: 91 mg

Total Carbohydrate: 4.8 g

Ingredients

1 lb – fresh lump crabmeat

2 Tbsp – mayonnaise

½ tsp – Worcestershire sauce

¼ tsp – fresh lemon juice

Black pepper to taste

Half cup – almond flour

2 tsp – green onion, finely chopped

1 – Egg

1 tsp – Dijon mustard

¼ tsp – hot sauce

1 ½ tsp – seafood seasoning

1 Tbsp – red pepper, finely chopped

1 Tbsp – fresh parsley, chopped

Cooking spray

Preparation Method

1. Coat a baking tray with cooking spray.
2. In a bowl, combine mayonnaise, Dijon mustard, egg, hot sauce, Worcestershire sauce, lemon juice, black pepper and seafood seasoning. Whisk well.
3. Fold the crab meat in this mixture. Make sure the meat is properly coated with this mixture.
4. Stir in peppers, parsley, green onions and half of the almond flour.
5. Divide this mixture in 6 equal parts. Form patty of every part.
6. Spread the remaining almond flour in a shallow bowl.
7. Dredge each patty in this floor and then place it on the greased baking tray.
8. Put the tray in the refrigerator to marinade for at least 1 hour.
9. Set the oven to preheat at 400°F.
10. Put the tray in the preheated oven for about 20 minutes or till the patties become golden brown.

Serve with any of the *Paleo Lunch Box Dips*.

Drunken Fish with Red Sauce

Serving Size

Serves 4

Nutritional Facts (Values per Serving)

Calories/Serving: 247

Protein: 29 g

Total Fat: 11 g

Cholesterol: 71 mg

Total Carbohydrate: 4 g

Ingredients

1 ¼ lb – tilapia

1 pint – cherry tomatoes, cut into halves

¼ tsp – black pepper

¼ cup – dry white wine

2 Tbsp – extra virgin olive oil

3 Tbsp – olive tapenade

3 – Garlic cloves, finely diced

¼ tsp – salt

Preparation Method

1. Season tilapia with salt and pepper.
2. Heat one tablespoon olive in a nonstick pan over medium-high heat.
3. Cook the seasoned fish in it for about 5 minutes or till it becomes golden brown, while flipping once in between.
4. Take it out in the serving platter.

5. In the same, combine the remaining olive oil, garlic, wine and tomatoes. Cover the pan and cook it on medium heat for 5 minutes, while stirring occasionally.

6. Add the olive tapenade. Cook and stir for one more minute.

7. Pour it over the fish and serve.

Spicy Sausage Burgers

Serving Size

Makes 8 patties

Nutritional Facts (Values per Serving)

Calories/Serving: 118

Protein: 10.1 g

Total Fat: 8.2 g

Cholesterol: 37 mg

Total Carbohydrate: 0.3 g

Ingredients

1 lb – ground pork

¾ tsp – ground black pepper

1 tsp – fresh thyme, finely chopped

¼ tsp – ground nutmeg

¼ tsp – red pepper flakes

2 tsp – fresh sage leaves, finely chopped

¼ tsp – fresh rosemary, chopped

¼ tsp – cayenne pepper

1 tsp – kosher salt

Preparation Method

1. In a large bowl, combine all the ingredients. Knead thoroughly with hands.
2. Divide the mixture into 8 equal parts and form 8 patties.
3. Heat a nonstick skillet over medium heat.
4. Cook patties in it for total 18 – 20 minutes or till browned, while flipping once in between.

Serve with hamburger buns and any of the *Paleo Lunch Box Dips*.

Melon and Pepper Grilled Shrimps

Serving Size

Serves 4

Nutritional Facts (Values per Serving)

Calories/Serving: 211

Protein: 19 g

Total Fat: 8 g

Cholesterol: 168 mg

Total Carbohydrate: 16 g

Ingredients

1 lb – raw shrimp, peeled and deveined

2 cups – finely chopped melon

2 Tbsp – fresh mint, finely chopped

2 tsp – ginger, finely grated, divided

1 cup – finely chopped fresh pineapple

4 – Romaine leaves

2 Tbsp – canola oil

1 – Small sized red onion, finely chopped

1 – Lime, cut into 4 wedges

2 tsp – minced jalapeno, divided

¼ cup – finely chopped red bell pepper

3 Tbsp – rice vinegar

¼ cup – finely chopped green bell pepper

½ tsp – sea salt

Preparation Method

1. In a bowl, combine shrimp, 1 tablespoon oil, 1 tsp jalapeno and 1 tsp ginger. Mix well.

2. Cover the bowl and put it in the refrigerator to marinade for at least 4 hours (maximum 24 hours).

3. In another bowl, combine pineapple, red bell pepper, green bell pepper, melon, onion, mint, salt, vinegar and the remaining oil. Mix well, cover and put it in the refrigerator for 30 minutes (maximum 4 hours).

4. Preheat the grill to high prior 20 minutes to serving.

5. Thread the marinated shrimps into skewers. While doing so, make sure you pierce each shrimp twice, from both ends.

6. Grill the shrimp for 3 minutes or until cooked through.

7. Set aside to cool for 10 minutes.

8. Slide the shrimp off the skewers and divide them into 4 equal parts.

9. Take four serving plates. Spread one leaf on each plate. Spoon the melon pineapple sauce over it. Place one part of the shrimps over the sauce. Garnish each plate with a lime wedge and serve.

Sweet Paleo Lunchbox

Choco Coconut Smoothie

Serving Size

Serves 9 – 10

Nutritional Facts (Values per Serving)

Calories/Serving: 151

Protein: 1.7 g

Total Fat: 9.3 g

Cholesterol: 0 mg

Total Carbohydrate: 19.8 g

Ingredients

2 – Avocados, peeled and pitted

2 Tbsp – coconut oil

Half cup – cocoa powder

1 tsp – vanilla essence

Half cup – honey

½ tsp – kosher salt

Coconut flakes to garnish

Preparation Method

1. Except for coconut flakes, combine all the other ingredients in food processor.
2. Blend till it becomes a smooth smoothie.
3. Pour it into serving glasses or bowls.
4. Garnish with coconut flakes and serve.

Apple 'n' Cranberries Cookies

Serving Size

Makes 24 cookies

Nutritional Facts (Values per Serving)

Calories/Serving: 159

Protein: 4.4 g

Total Fat: 10.4 g

Cholesterol: 16 mg

Total Carbohydrate: 14.1 g

Ingredients

2 cups – unsweetened applesauce

3 cups – almond flour

Half cup – pecans, chopped

2 – Eggs, beaten

2 tsp – cinnamon powder

1 ½ tsp – baking soda

Half cup – crystallized sugar cane juice

Half cup – dried cranberries

¼ cup – coconut flour

2 tsp – cake spice

Cooking spray

Preparation Method

1. Set the oven to preheat at 400°F.

2. Line baking tray with parchment paper and then grease it with cooking spray.

3. In a large bowl, combine applesauce and baking soda. Mix till the baking soda dissolves.

4. Stir in almond flour, chopped pecans, crystallized sugar cane juice, eggs, dried cranberries, cinnamon powder, coconut flour and cake spice. Mix well.

5. Place spoonfuls of this dough on the prepared baking tray, at least 2 inches apart each other.

6. Put it in the preheated oven for about 15 minutes or until set.

Cashew Date Cookies

Serving Size

Makes 8 cookies

Nutritional Facts (Values per Serving)

Calories/Serving: 160

Protein: 4.3 g

Total Fat: 11.7 g

Cholesterol: 26 mg

Total Carbohydrate: 12 g

Ingredients

1 Tbsp – honey

Half cup – cashew butter

4 – Pitted dates, chopped

¼ cup – dried cranberries

1 Tbsp – coconut oil

¼ cup – chopped almonds

1 – Egg

Cooking spray

Preparation Method

1. Set the oven to preheat at 350°F.
2. Coat a baking tray with cooking spray.
3. In a large bowl, combine all the ingredients. Mix well.
4. Place spoonfuls on the prepared baking tray, at least 2 inches apart each other.
5. Put it in the preheated oven for about 12 minutes or until set.

6. Let the cookies cool and harden for a while. Serve.

5-minute Ovenless Muffins

Serving Size

Makes 2 muffins

Nutritional Facts (Values per Serving)

Calories/Serving: 285

Protein: 20.1 g

Total Fat: 18.4 g

Cholesterol: 212 mg

Total Carbohydrate: 13.8 g

Ingredients

2 Tbsp – flax seed meal

½ tsp – coconut oil

¼ tsp – baking powder

¼ cup – almond flour

1 – Egg

½ tsp – cinnamon powder

Pinch of kosher salt

Preparation Method

1. Grease two microwave safe ramekins with oil or cooking spray.
2. In a bowl, combine all the ingredients. Mix well.
3. Divide the mixture equally in the two greased ramekins.
4. Microwave for 30 seconds. Let it sit for 5 seconds. Microwave again for 30 seconds or till the muffins rise and are cooked through.

Serve!

Choco Banana Loaf

Serving Size

Serves 8

Nutritional Facts (Values per Serving)

Calories/Serving: 355

Protein: 8.9 g

Total Fat: 22.7 g

Cholesterol: 110 mg

Total Carbohydrate: 35.6 g

Ingredients

4 – Eggs

1 cup – semi sweet chocolate chips

1 tsp – coconut oil

1 cup – mashed bananas

1 tsp – baking soda

Half cup – almond butter

1 Tbsp – unsalted butter, softened

1 Tbsp – cinnamon powder

Half cup – coconut flour

Pinch of sea salt

Cooking spray

Preparation Method

1. Set the oven to preheat at 350°F.
2. Coat a 9x5 inches loaf pan with cooking spray.

3. Melt unsalted butter, chocolate chips and 1 tsp coconut oil in microwave or in a double boiler over simmering water. Stir in cinnamon powder.

4. In another large bowl, sift together baking soda, flour and salt. Mix well.

5. Fold it into the mashed bananas.

6. In another bowl, combine almond butter and eggs. Beat till it becomes smooth and creamy. Add this mixture into the banana mixture. Mix well.

7. Pour half of this batter into the prepared loaf pan.

8. Spread half of the chocolate mixture over it.

9. Top it up with the remaining batter followed by the remaining chocolate mixture.

10. Put it in the preheated oven for 50 minutes or till cooked through.

11. Set aside to cool for 10 minutes.

12. Slice and serve.

Lemon 'n' Date Tarts

Serving Size

Serves 4

Nutritional Facts (Values per Serving)

Calories/Serving: 244

Protein: 9.5 g

Total Fat: 16.5 g

Cholesterol: 106 mg

Total Carbohydrate: 19.9 g

Ingredients for Tart Crust

3 Tbsp – fresh lemon juice

1 cup – almond meal

4 – Pitted dates

Ingredients for Tart Filling

2 – Eggs

6 Tbsp – fresh lemon juice

1 Tbsp – honey

2 tsp – lemon zest

Preparation Method

1. Set the oven to preheat at 350°F.
2. Place paper liners in four cupcake cups.
3. Combine the tart crust ingredients in a food processor. Blend till all the ingredients are thoroughly combined.
4. Press the crust mixture evenly and firmly into the bottom and up the sides of the paper-lined cupcake cups.

5. Put it in the preheated oven for 10 minutes or till the crust become golden brown.

Meanwhile, make the filling. To make the tart filling,

6. Heat lemon juice, honey and lemon zest in a saucepan.

7. Bring it to simmer over low heat.

8. Beat eggs in a bowl and then slowly add them in the saucepan while whisking fast and constantly.

9. When all the eggs are thoroughly mixed, remove the saucepan off the heat.

10. Set aside to cool for 5 minutes.

11. Pour it into the baked crusts.

12. Put the tarts in the refrigerator for about 20 minutes and then serve.

Paleo Almond Bites

Serving Size

Serves 10 – 12

Nutritional Facts (Values per Serving)

Calories/Serving: 90

Protein: 8.4 g

Total Fat: 3.5 g

Cholesterol: 0.1 mg

Total Carbohydrate: 8 g

Ingredients

2 cups – almond meal

3 – Egg whites

1 ½ tsp – cinnamon powder

½ tsp – ground nutmeg

1 ½ tsp – Honey

Preparation Method

1. Set the oven to preheat at 350°F.
2. Line a baking tray with parchment paper.
3. In a bowl, combine honey, almond meal, nutmeg and cinnamon.
4. Beat the egg whites till it becomes stiff.
5. Fold it in the almond meal mixture.
6. Place spoonfuls on the prepared baking tray, at least 2 inches apart each other.
7. Put it in the preheated oven for about 15 minutes or until browned.

Fruit and Nut Bars

Serving Size

Makes 18 – 20 bars

Nutritional Facts (Values per Serving)

Calories/Serving: 356

Protein: 12.5 g

Total Fat: 25.2 g

Cholesterol: 0.2 mg

Total Carbohydrate: 25.4 g

Ingredients

1 cup – pecans

1 cup – pumpkin seeds

1 cup – protein powder, vanilla flavored

Half cup – raisins

¼ cup – maple syrup

1 Tbsp – vanilla essence

1 ½ tsp – molasses

2 cups – walnuts

2 cups – almonds

1 cup – dried cranberries

Half cup – pitted dates

Half cup – coconut flour

3 Tbsp – coconut oil

1 ½ tsp – cinnamon powder

Cooking spray

Preparation Method

1. Set the oven to preheat at 220°F.
2. Spread the walnuts and pecans on a nonstick baking pan.
3. Bake the nuts for 30 minutes or till the nuts are roasted.
4. Carefully take the roasted nuts tray out of the oven and set it aside.
5. Increase the oven temperature to 230°F.
6. Coat a 9x13 inches pan with cooking spray.
7. Combine the roasted walnuts, almonds and roasted pecans in a food processor.
8. Pulse till all the nuts are coarsely chopped and combined.
9. Take it out in a large bowl.
10. Stir in the cranberries, pitted dates, pumpkin seeds, protein powder, raisins, maple syrup, coconut flour, coconut oil, cinnamon powder, vanilla essence and molasses. Mix well.
11. Press the mixture into the greased baking pan.
12. Put the pan in the preheated oven for 40 minutes or till it becomes golden brown.
13. Set aside to cool for 10 minutes.
14. Slice and serve.

Fruity Coffee Cake

Serving Size

Makes 1 standard size cake (approximately 8 servings)

Nutritional Facts (Values per Serving)

Calories/Serving: 528

Protein: 10 g

Total Fat: 35.4 g

Cholesterol: 178 mg

Total Carbohydrate: 48.2 g

Ingredients for Topping

2 oz. – unsalted butter, cut into 1 inch cubes

¾ cup – walnuts, chopped

1 tsp – cinnamon powder

3 Tbsp – raw honey

2 Tbsp – coconut flour

Ingredients for Filling

1 – Apple, peeled and thinly sliced

4 oz. – soft unsalted butter

5 – Eggs

¾ cup – coconut milk

1 tsp – vanilla essence

½ tsp – baking soda

2 – Pears, peeled and thinly sliced

2 tsp – fresh lemon juice

¼ cup – raw honey

¾ cup – coconut flour

¼ cup – arrowroot powder

¾ tsp – baking powder

½ tsp – sea salt

Preparation Method

1. Set the oven to preheat at 350°F.
2. Wrap the base of a springform pan with aluminum foil and then grease the pan with cooking spray or melted coconut oil.
3. In a bowl, mix together walnuts, cinnamon powder and 3 Tbsp honey. Set aside.
4. In another bowl, combine butter cubes and 2 Tbsp coconut flour. Mix till it becomes a crumbly mixture.
5. Stir in the walnut-honey mixture.
6. In another bowl, mix together apples, pears and lemon juice. Set aside.
7. In another large mixing bowl, combine half cup softened unsalted butter, eggs and ¼ cup honey. Beat well.
8. Whisk in coconut milk, arrowroot powder, baking powder, vanilla essence, baking soda, coconut flour and sea salt.
9. Pout half of this batter into the prepared springform pan.
10. Spread the pear-apple mixture over it.
11. Pour over the remaining batter.
12. Top it up with the walnut mixture.
13. Put it in the preheated oven for about 50 minutes or till a toothpick when inserted in the middle of the cake comes out clean.
14. Set aside to cool for 10 minutes.
15. Take it out of the pan and allow it to cool for 60 minutes.

Slice and serve.

Applesauce Cupcakes

Serving Size

Make 12 cupcakes

Nutritional Facts (Values per Serving)

Calories/Serving: 197

Protein: 2 g

Total Fat: 11.6 g

Cholesterol: 53 mg

Total Carbohydrate: 21.7 g

Ingredients

Half cup – applesauce

1 Tbsp – almond milk

Half cup – coconut oil, melted

3 Tbsp – honey

Half cup – coconut flour

¼ tsp – baking soda

Half cup – raspberry jam

3 – Eggs

3 Tbsp – vanilla essence

½ tsp – sea salt

Preparation Method

1. Set the oven to preheat at 350°F.
2. Place paper liners in cupcake cups.
3. Combine applesauce, eggs, coconut oil, honey and vanilla essence in a food processor. Blend till all the ingredients are thoroughly combined.

4. Take it out in a large bowl.

5. Stir in salt, coconut flour and baking soda. Mix well.

6. Stir in almond milk.

7. Pour out the batter in the paper-lined cups while filling 2/3 of each cup.

8. Swirl the raspberry jam over it.

9. Put it in the preheated oven for about 25 minutes or till a toothpick when inserted in the middle of the cupcake comes out clean.